SHEARER

Neridah McMullin

Michael Tomkins

WALKER BOOKS
AND SUBSIDIARIES
LONDON • BOSTON • SYDNEY • AUCKLAND

Jack Howe had
hands the size of tennis racquets,
legs like tree trunks
and wrists made of steel.

Despite his size, he was light on his feet and did an excellent Irish jig.

But what Jack was really good at was shearing sheep.

Jack's hand blade was like an extension of himself. He sheared sheep neatly with precision and grace. He was **lightning fast** …

and he **never** nicked them with the blade.

One Saturday morning in the woolshed, when the shearers were counting up their sheep tallies after the first two-hour run, another ringer, Bluey McGee **scoffed** at him:

'Mate, is that the best you can do? I heard you were a gun.'

Jack smiled.

The bell rang for the next run and the blade in Jack's hands **flew** through the fleece. It was warm in the shed and the sheep **wriggled** like grubs. Jack found himself so hot, he tore the sleeves off his shirt.

He put his head down
and kept on shearing.

On a typical Saturday morning, shearing **100** sheep was normal, but that day Jack sheared **144** sheep! When the bell rang at knock off, he stood up to find all the workers in the shed clapping him – he'd set a **new record**.

'I mighta **underestimated** ya, mate,' grinned Bluey.

Word travelled of Jack's feat and a **shearing competition** was announced. The search was on to find the **world's greatest shearer.** There was a gold medal on offer and Jack had his eye on it.

'You can't shear 300 sheep in one day, mate. No-one can,' said Bluey.

Jack smiled.

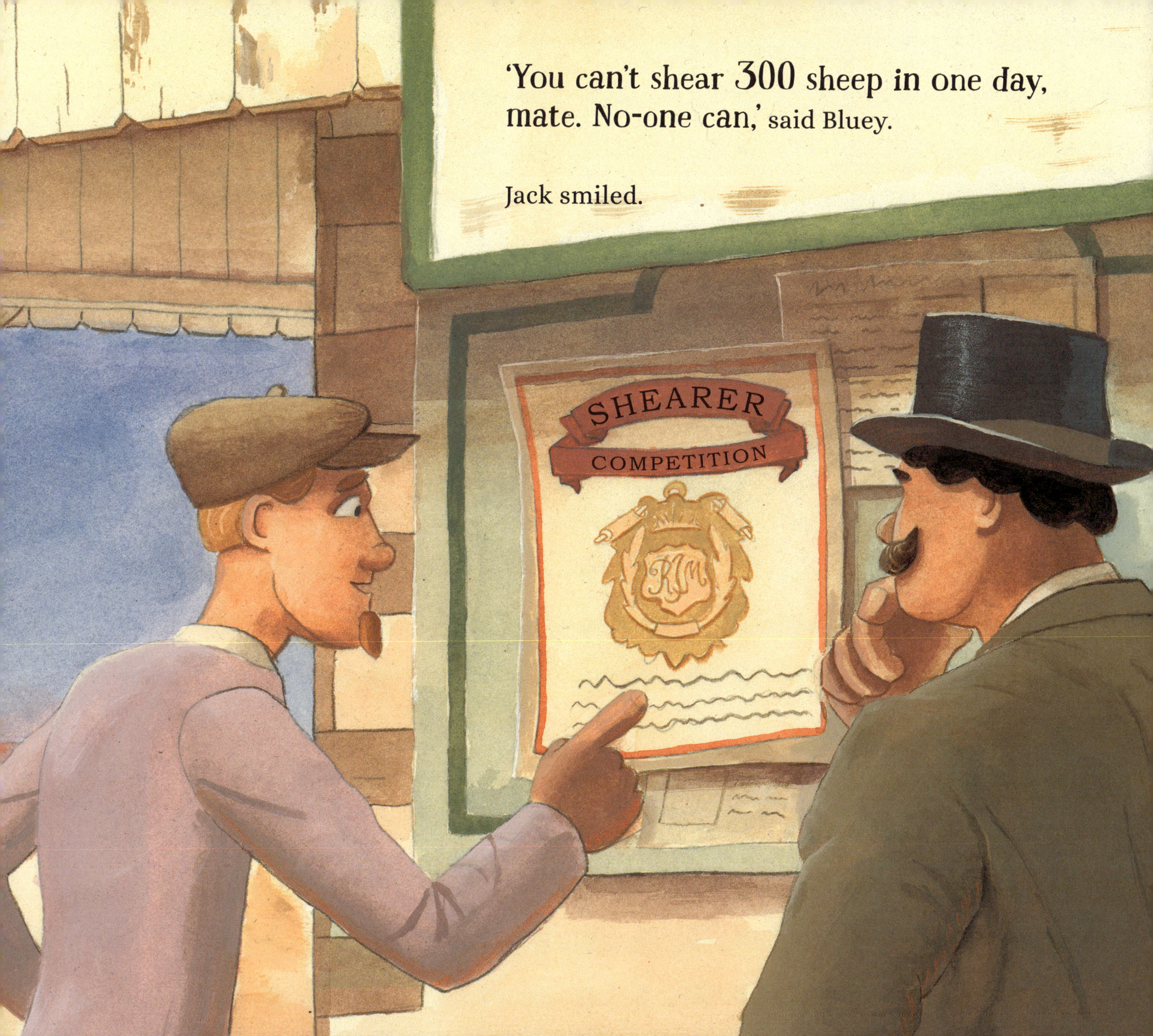

The competition was held at Alice Downs Station. The shearers stood on the board waiting to get their first sheep. Dogs barked and sheep bleated as stockmen put the last of the sheep in the yards.

The stink of lanolin and wool and tar wafted through the air.

The Boss stared down the line. He rang the bell and the sounds of **snipping** and **clipping** filled the air.

There were **tar boys, rouseabouts, wool classers, stockmen** and **squatters** all crowded around to watch.

Jack set a sizzling pace and as the day wore on, everyone expected him to slow down. But he didn't.

Jack was shearing **even faster.**

Jack clipped around the head of the sheep, and delicately shaved their legs, sweeping the blade smoothly along their backs with the long blow.

People watched wide-eyed.

Jack fleeced the flock so swiftly, even the sheep looked stunned.

'Go, Jack!' everyone shouted.

'You little ripper, Jack!'

As Jack neared the record of 300 sheep,

Terry Downes sidled onto the board . . .

and **jumped** up onto Jack's back!

But Jack **didn't miss a beat.**

Some joker kept putting sheared sheep **back** into his catching pens, trying to slow him down —

but it didn't stop Jack.
His wrists flicked
and his muscles flexed,
his hands were a speedy blur.

Kevie McClennan ambled up to Jack and started **tickling** him under his arms.

Jack didn't even crack a grin. He just kept on shearing.

Jack was **unstoppable**, and he left his competition far behind.

After 300 sheep, Jack had broken the record but he kept on shearing. The crowd begged him to stop — they wanted to celebrate.

But it was only after he'd
sheared his 321st sheep,
that Jack put down his blade,
wiped his brow
and put the last sheep
gently into its pen.

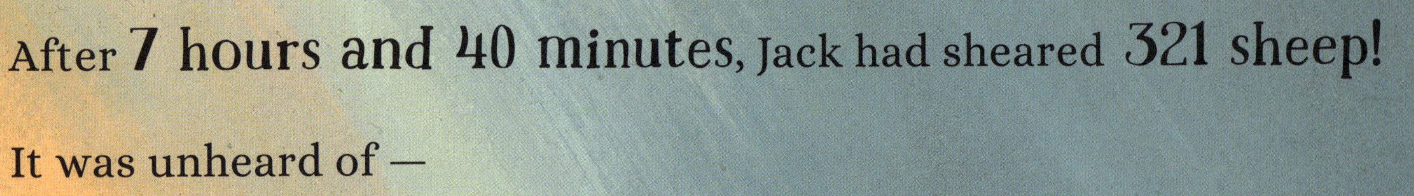

After 7 hours and 40 minutes, Jack had sheared 321 sheep!

It was unheard of –

Jack was the shearing Champion of Australia,

the Colonies

and the **WORLD!**

There were handshakes all round. Everyone wanted to know Jack, and everyone wanted him shearing in *their* sheds.

'Come on, Jack! Come and celebrate!' they cried.

Jack shook his head and smiled.
'Sorry, lads. Gotta go.'

And he left the shed with **a pirouette** and a wave of his hand.

First published in 2023
by Walker Books Australia Pty Ltd
Locked Bag 22, Newtown
NSW 2042 Australia
www.walkerbooks.com.au

This edition published in 2025

Walker Books acknowledges the Traditional Owners of the country on which we work, the Gadigal and Wangal peoples of the Eora Nation, and recognises their continuing connection to the land, waters and culture. We pay our respect to their Elders past and present.

NATIONAL LIBRARY OF AUSTRALIA

A catalogue record for this book is available from the National Library of Australia

ISBN: 978 1 761601 67 5

The illustrations for this book were created using watercolour and gouache
Typeset in Alice and Mrs Ant
Printed and bound in China
EU Authorized Representative: HackettFlynn Ltd, 36 Cloch Choirneal, Balrothery, Co. Dublin, K32 C942, Ireland. EU@walkerpublishinggroup.com

10 9 8 7 6 5 4 3 2 1

TO JACK HOWE AND ALL SHEARERS PAST AND PRESENT – N.M.

FOR MY LOVE GEORGINA, AND MY CAT TOASTY – THE TEAM – M.T.

Born in Darling Downs in Queensland in 1861, **Jack Howe** set a hand-blade shearing record that remains unbeaten. Jack was a giant of a man. He was quite the athlete, winning a 100-yard sprint on a grass track in his socks in 11 seconds flat. He'd also won prizes at competitions for dancing the Irish jig.

In the 1880s, the wool industry was booming and it was the most important product to the Australian economy. Shearing is a backbreaking job. The blades in those early days were similar to a pair of scissors. The shearers were, and still are, paid for the number of sheep they shear in four two-hourly runs, creating strong competition to get the largest tally for the day. Jack's presence in a shearing shed lifted tallies far above normal as men tried to compete with him.

Sheep were shorn by hand blades until 1892, when a new technology, mechanised hand pieces, was invented by Mr. Fred Wolseley. After Jack won the Blade Shearing Championship, he went on to master mechanised shearing, and he won that title too! He used and promoted the new technology for Fred Wolseley until he retired in 1901.

When Jack tore the sleeves off his shirt, his mother converted all his flannels into 'singlets'. This fad took hold and, before long, all the shearers were wearing sleeveless flannels. A manufacturer also caught on and started making lighter cotton singlets and so the 'athletic singlet' was born, known as a 'Jack Howe' singlet. Today, it is known as the branded Bonds singlet.

Jack Howe was a supporter of workers unions and a lifelong Labor Party member. When dressed in a suit, Jack always wore his medals and a watch on a fob chain.

While Jack's story as told in this book is true, some names of other characters have been fictionalised.